N.º 1068 (1.)
Sͭ L.

N.º 1069 (1.)
R.

N.º 1070 (1.)
B.

N.º 1071 (1)

m.ᵉ sablée et fleurons.

m.ᵉ sablée et arabesque.

m.ᵉ carré de diamants et filets.

franges et filets.

Verres en tulipe.

Sͭ L.

1074 (1)

B.

1075 (1)

B. et Sͭ L.

1076 (1)

B.

m.ᵉ sablée et diamants.

m.ᵉ sablée et arabesque.

m.ᵉ à palmes de diamants.

m.ᵉ carrés de diam.ᵗˢ et filets

N.º 1080 (2.)
B et Sͭ L.

N.º 1081 (2) Sͭ L.

N.º 1083 (2)
Sͭ L.

N.º 1084 (1)
Sͭ L.

Verre gondole à bouton
sans taille.

m.ᵉ à diamants et feuille

Verre en gondole jambe balustre.

m.ᵉ à diamants bivaux

Verre ballon

m.ᵉ sablée et fleurons.

Verre conique sans taille.

EVERYDAY THINGS™
glass

SUZANNE SLESIN
DANIEL ROZENSZTROCH
STAFFORD CLIFF

↓

PHOTOGRAPHS BY MARIE-PIERRE MOREL
HARRY N. ABRAMS, INC., PUBLISHERS

EVERYDAY THINGS™
glass

SUZANNE SLESIN

DANIEL ROZENSZTROCH

STAFFORD CLIFF

PHOTOGRAPHS BY MARIE-PIERRE MOREL

HARRY N. ABRAMS, INC., PUBLISHERS

contents

contents

OPPOSITE This dark green glass jar for preserves with an archaic sealing system is an early-twentieth-century example.

THIS PAGE Molded nineteenth-century cologne bottles came in varying green hues.

preface

With the exception of the invention of the glass-pressing machine in the 1820s in America, the artisanal techniques of glassmaking have changed very little in the last two thousand years. Even in antiquity, the production of blown glass was significant, and glass objects made for domestic life were widely used in Roman times.

Early European glassmakers were itinerant craftspeople, but by the seventeenth century, France could count more than three thousand glassblowers who had established themselves in towns and villages. By 1800, the Normandy and Lorraine regions were the well-known centers of French glassmaking. Similarities between European and American blown and molded glass abounded as immigrants to the New World brought with them not only their possessions but also their skills and traditions.

However, it was not until the end of the eighteenth century that an efflorescence in glassblowing and molding was reflected in the large variety of domestic glass objects. Innovations of the period—such as the invention in the 1830s of the three-mold technique for which Sandwich Glass of Massachusetts became famous—are still admired today.

The early craftsmen in the Sandwich factory, founded in 1825, came from England. The factory produced an impressive number of bowls, dishes, vases, and even pharmaceutical wares. But the fragility of these utilitarian pieces, and the fact that they were used on a regular basis in home kitchens, restaurants, and shops make them rare nowadays, in spite of the quantities in which they once existed.

Today, we are attracted to the lightness of blown-glass pieces, but also to the imperfections that make each piece unique; to the geometric motifs and rich colors of pressed glass; and to the grandiose molded shapes of carafes, pitchers, and shallow covered bowls. These useful glass objects are truly timeless. Although they reflect the past, they are not nostalgic and old-fashioned. Rather, they are of our time, and easily take their place in the most contemporary of environments.

LEFT The Corning Glass Works' heat-resistant Pyrex, invented in 1915, serves as a double boiler that dates from the forties.

The earliest glass nursing bottles were hand or mold blown and could be sterilized. This unusual one with two openings—one for a nipple, one for a rubber stopper—was devised in England around 1900, and similar examples were still in use in the 1950s. Today, it has become a dramatic vase for a single sculptural flower.

LEFT Molded conical-shaped glass string holders were conveniently kept on store counters. A hole in the top allowed the string spooled inside to be easily pulled out for wrapping packages.

RIGHT An enormous molded-glass goblet both displayed and advertised a chocolate stick candy.

LEFT Blow-molded, paneled Sandwich Glass salt shakers have metal screw caps and "agitators" to keep the salt from caking. They were patented in 1877.

RIGHT This unusual shallow molded-glass footed cup for serving brandied fruit has a solid glass bowl.

LEFT This molded glass bottle with a stopper was used for blessing church congregants with holy water.

RIGHT Nineteenth-century yellow-green molded glass, like this candlestick, is referred to as Vaseline glass because its hue closely resembles the petroleum jelly of the same name. The statuette of the Madonna is a cast plaster multiple by German conceptual artist Katharina Fritsch.

LEFT A fine example of early
Sandwich Glass, this cobalt
blue lead three-mold-blown
decanter dates from the 1830s.

OPPOSITE Footed blown-glass
bowls usually held sucking
leeches for medicinal purposes,
or goldfish.

TO DRINK

The drinking glass has always been synonymous with bistro culture, wh

Glasses
Pitchers
Bottles

essitated having many different glasses of varying sizes. Each drink, whether absinthe, wine, beer, cider, lemonade, or even coffee, was served in its own glass and poured from a particular, and sometimes graduated, carafe. The typical ware was hardy enough to support the repeated shocks of café life—whether clinking glasses on zinc counters or repeated washings. Glass manufacturers offered thousands of molded or blow-molded glasses, mugs, goblets, pitchers, and bottles. Illustrated catalogs that appeared in the nineteenth century in France, Germany, and England testified to the importance of the new glass industry. In America, in the 1820s and 1830s, companies such as Sandwich Glass reflected the European traditions of blow-molding glass. The development of glass-pressing that allowed for the emulation of sought-after cut and blown European designs satisfied the demands of the growing middle class.

LEFT Blown and molded two-quart carafes, like this one with subtle facets, were originally used in restaurants to serve water, lemonade, or table wine. The pressed late-nineteenth-century footed wine goblet from Pennsylvania is in a popular pattern called "Egg in Sand."

RIGHT This French pressed-glass carafe, with a stopper stamped "Orangeade Terrier" and a decorative flower pattern in the fashionable Art Nouveau style, was made as an advertising premium for a well-known orange syrup company. The pressed-glass footed goblet, marked 1876 and decorated with the Liberty Bell, commemorates 100 years of American Independence.

During the 1950s, a glass factory in Piraeus, near Athens, manufactured numerous carafes in varying shades of blue that were meant to serve Ouzo, the popular anise-flavored Greek drink. Here they have a new life by a stone sink and on a mantelpiece in a Cycladic Islands summer house.

Glass wine bottles were blown in many of the famous wine regions of France and had different dark hues depending on the minerals used in their creation. Beginning in the sixteenth and seventeenth centuries, thick bottles were used specifically for carrying wine from the barrel to the table. By the nineteenth century, wine was being transported by train in glass bottles, and production intensified until glass was widely mass produced.

Small French blow-molded clear carafes for serving spirits in bistros were often etched, either with markings that showed how much a customer had consumed, left, or with the proprietor's monogram, right. The shallow footed glass, at left, is of the type specifically used for serving cherries or plums in eau de vie or brandy. The small thick glass, at right, holds a standard measure for a single shot of alcohol.

LEFT Small, squat, heavy tumblers that had dispropor - tionately large bases but held very little are known as "thief's glasses" or "fake bottoms." Bartenders customarily used them to clink glasses with customers without consuming in excess.

RIGHT Throughout Greece, shapely carafes and scalloped glass plates are still found in taverns today. They are used to serve the traditional ouzo along with *meze*, small salty snacks such as olives, capers, and anchovies.

ABOVE In Greece, ouzo is either
served from an individual carafe
or poured directly into a tall,
pressed glass. Cold water—
brought to the table in large
handled pitchers—can be added
to dilute and stretch the drink.

RIGHT Small blown and molded
pitchers made for serving cider
or wine are available in many
different patterns.

Four-quart carafes for lemonade,
like the one shown at center,
and basic blown-glass pitchers
for dispensing water, wine, and
cider were café basics.

LEFT Although once widely available in many different patterns and sizes, French cider and lemonade pitchers and jugs, with elongated shapes and pressed geometric designs, have become rare.

RIGHT Cider carafes are typical of Normandy, the region in France known for its apples and a centuries-old tradition of cider production.

Handled tankards and mugs for beer, left, or coffee and hot toddies, right, made their appearance in the nineteenth century. Early mugs were handmade and irregular, as in the unusual early-nineteenth-century Austrian example at left. Mass-produced versions, like those at right, were commonplace by the end of the last century.

LEFT Tall tumblers, many made in the glass factories of eastern France, appeared on the counters and tables of every brasserie. Vintage catalogs show myriad variations on the basic shape.

RIGHT Overscaled pitchers were traditionally used in French brasseries to serve lemonade. When lemonade is added to beer, the result is an Alsatian classic known as a *panaché*.

BELOW Handled blow-molded beer tankards, with flat facets or raised round bubble-shaped patterns, have been popular since the sixteenth century. Their shape is derived from pewter or ironstone mugs that often had covers to keep the beer warm, the way it was drunk in the past.

OPPOSITE These footed, molded beer mugs have the raised motifs of glasses made by companies such as Etablissement de Portieux in the Vosges region of eastern France.

LEFT By the end of the nineteenth century there was a particular glass for every type of drink served in bistros. Footed glasses, top row, known as *mazagrans*, had thick walls to keep coffee hot. Glasses for absinthe, a mixture of different plant extracts and alcohol that was forbidden after 1915, had a typically thick conical shape, bottom row left. The absinthe was poured in the glass over a cube of sugar that was placed on the accompanying spoon. In the villages of Slovakia, hand-blown goblets were often etched in honor of special occasions, such as births and weddings, bottom row right.

RIGHT This wine glass, etched with the name of a grocery in a tiny village of France, was given out as a premium item.

Inspired by the cut-crystal glassware of Bohemia, which was fashionable in the mid-nineteenth century, many French glassmakers, such as the Etablissement de Porthieu or the Cristallerie du Creusot, created their own pressed-glass versions in amber and blue.

Goblets made for displaying
violets are sought after
among glass collectors.
Examples in certain hues, like
the amethyst one shown here,
left, are harder to find, as are
the more elaborately shaped
and decorated pieces.

The home kitchen of the past, with its traditional recipes and season

TO EAT

Jars, Cruets, Canisters

2

thms of jam-making, canning, and pickling, required a multitude of containers of different sizes, in which a variety of fruits and vegetables as well as oil, vinegar, and more exotic condiments could be preserved over time. Glass, because of its hygienic properties, whether hand-blown eighteenth-century jam jars or the nostalgic milk bottles that were on every doorstep before breakfast, has long been eminently suitable—and aesthetically appetizing—for storing and presenting food. The marble counters of dairy shops, drugstore counters, and the well-worn wood tables of old-fashioned general stores were the perfect stage for overscaled canisters and footed bowls filled with fresh eggs or candy. Colorful Depression glass, opaque milk glass, and translucent Vaseline glass further expanded the vocabulary of everyday glass.

During the summer and fall, keeping honey, making jellies, and preserving jams made from ripe seasonal fruits were common practices in every old-fashioned household. Glass jars of all kinds were filled with glistening jams and stored in pantries to be consumed during the following year. The pressed grape-patterned jam pot, top row left, and tiny blow-molded jam jar, reserved for the last spoonfuls, bottom row left, are typically French. The delicate eighteenth-century blown-glass jam dish with its saucer and cover, bottom row right, was for serving preserves in a more elegant fashion. The pressed-glass mold, top row right, allowed for the creation of fanciful jellies. A blown-glass jar from the eighteenth century, right, shows off the translucence of honey.

Brandied paper covers were tied to the rims of French eighteenth-century hand-blown jam pots to help in the preservation of the cooked fruit.

These pressed and molded
American maple syrup
pitchers, with tin lids and
applied handles, date from
about 1880 to 1910. The
vintage pressed-glass honey
pot is English.

A French eighteenth-century
footed blown-glass bowl used
to hold sugar or jam.

These American Fry opalescent ovenproof custard cups date from 1927.

In the eighteenth century, mustards and other condiments were sold throughout the French countryside by itinerant vendors. By the middle of the nineteenth century, the artisanal production had been industrialized, and by 1900 the town of Dijon, France, became synonymous with mustard. The condiment began to be sold in blow-molded glass jars embossed with the makers' names—an early foray into commercial packaging—which replaced the traditional ironstone pots.

In the last quarter of the nineteenth century, inventors and manufacturers such as Masons, Leotric, and Atlas vied for patents on inventive methods to improve the hermetic seal of canning jars.

LEFT This early Millville, New Jersey, fruit jar dates from about 1862. An iron yoke and thumbscrew secures the glass lid.

RIGHT Vintage green patented canning jars, either with metal screw tops or glass lids held with wire, are more apt to be used today as storage canisters than for canning.

LEFT A variety of French canning jars existed to preserve different products. The barrel-shaped molded jar, top row left, was for vegetables. Jars marked L'Idéale, bottom row left, with their patented porcelain stoppers, came in many sizes. The elongated blown-glass jar, top row right, is from the eighteenth century and was specially made to preserve precious truffles. The wide-mouthed, dark-green blown-glass jar was for preserving cornichons, or small pickles, in vinegar.

RIGHT It was common practice on farms in Provence to cut bunches of slightly unripe grapes and store them in blown-glass jars. This old-fashioned preservation technique would allow the fruit to ripen slowly and be enjoyed at a later time.

LEFT This tiny blown-glass jar still has the wire handle with which it was lowered into boiling water during the canning process.

RIGHT A Milanese glass collector's kitchen shelves display a variety of unusual pieces of vintage blown glass that she brought back from her forays to flea markets all over the world.

ABOVE An American Squirrel Brand molded-glass jar with a peanut-shaped finial on the lid and cheerful yellow graphics boasted the quality of its peanuts.

RIGHT This lidded blown-glass jar once held sweets in a traditional French candy shop.

Transparent footed bowls, with domed or flat covers, are as appetizing for storing brioches or rock candy at home as they were in shops in the past.

The invention of Pyrex by the Corning Glass Works in 1915 expanded the cooking possibilities of glass. The addition of borosilicates allowed the glass to resist heat and thermal shocks. Over the decades, dozens of cooking items were introduced, including these now collectible—and still usable—glass-handled tea and coffee pots, above, and saucepan, right, that date from the 1940s.

These Japanese molded-glass bottles from the 1930s, originally for soy sauce, are now filled with olive oil and balsamic vinegar.

In a gourmet kitchen, the sophisticated expertise in a variety of oils and vinegars—for cooking and salad dressings—has revitalized vintage cruets. Double-sided, Venetian-inspired blown-glass cruets keep oil and vinegar separate yet together, top row left. Because of their fragility, it is difficult to find eighteenth-century blown-glass cruets with thin elongated spouts in perfect condition, bottom row.

Each of these eighteenth-century blown-glass cruets has its own elegant spout. The fineness of the glass contrasts with the rustic glazed tile and wood-handled knives in an Italian kitchen.

LEFT Mass-produced in large quantities, Depression-era glassware was once affordable and omnipresent in most American kitchens. The utilitarian pressed-glass wares have now become collectible. Clockwise from top left: lemon squeezer, Hocking Glass Company green transparent mixing bowls and paneled pitcher, Mr. Peanut-shaped salt and pepper shakers, and storage jars.

RIGHT This six-piece mold-blown colorless lead-glass castor set dates from about 1830. The three-mold geometric design was influenced by the cut glass that was in vogue at the time.

Milk glass, in production in America since the 1860s, was at first a stand-in for fine porcelain before taking on its own allure. Arsenic, and later tin oxide and feldspar, were added to the glass to achieve the desired whiteness. This patented 1930s orange squeezer, embossed with the Sunkist trademark, was sold by mail and in stores with Sunkist fruit.

These Scandinavian dairy dishes, now more than 200 years old, were once commonplace in every household. The thin blown glass was made into individual dishes, right, or large serving pieces equipped with spouts for easy pouring, above.

ABOVE AND RIGHT Small blown-glass bell jars are just the right size to protect cheese that should be served at room temperature.

FAR LEFT TOP This French 1950s baby bottle from Nestlé promoted concentrated milk.

FAR LEFT BOTTOM Turn-of-the-last-century French milk bottles were equipped with glass stoppers and wire handles that allowed them to be carried and refilled at the dairy shop.

LEFT TOP, LEFT BOTTOM, AND RIGHT In America and England, milk and cream used to be delivered daily to people's doorsteps in consigned bottles, often marked with the name of the dairy.

OPPOSITE An American glass milk bottle is now an amusing breakfast jug at a summer house in the Greek Islands.

ABOVE Porcelain-and-tin caps with rubber seals allowed French milk bottles to be airtight.

LEFT In the past, food items were often displayed under large and heavy blown-glass cloches on the counters of cheese shops and grocery stores. The huge ten-quart blown-glass jar, with its spout and handle, was probably used to dispense olive oil after the pressing.

THIS PAGE Thick and solid, nineteenth-century footed blown-glass bowls in which fresh eggs were displayed were once found in every small-town dairy shop.

LEFT A vintage pressed-glass English toast rack and chunky American eggcups (the one at center can be turned upside down for soft-boiled or poached eggs) are as convenient at breakfast time today as they were many decades ago.

RIGHT Lidded containers from the 1940s were originally used to store food in the early refrigerators that revolutionized the modern American kitchen. Today, the all-purpose boxes are no longer hidden away but can take pride of place in full view on the kitchen counter.

LEFT Small plates, either pressed or molded, are decorative and functional additions to any table. Greek dishes, left top and bottom, are for savory appetizers or sweet fruit preserves. Blown three-mold American Sandwich glass plates and shallow bowls have a geometric pattern and date from the early nineteenth century, right top. A turn-of-the-last-century plate with an intricate pressed design mimics cut crystal, right bottom.

RIGHT These American pressed dessert plates have the popular sheaf-of-wheat pattern that was originally seen on milk glass.

LEFT By the 1880s, pressed glass came in a range of colors that satisfied the demands of a growing public. Yellow-green glass, known as Vaseline glass because it resembled the petroleum jelly of the same name, was common. The small stand, top, was once a grocery-shop display for Teaberry Gum. The shallow-footed bowl, bottom, once at home in the Victorian kitchen, has now moved to the dining table.

RIGHT American clear-glass footed compote and cookie stands have simple, classic shapes that have stood the test of time.

Over the past 150 years, there have been few occupations in which glass did not play

TO RE-USE

Test Tubes, Beakers

portant role. Scientific experimentation brought about the creation of fanciful and eccentric paraphernalia. Doctors rarely paid house calls without prescribing the application of vacuum cups. Firemen relied on molded-glass gas-filled grenades to help extinguish flames. The lacemaker continued to work as night fell thanks to the ingenious magnification of candlelight through colored water. Fishermen tied colored blown-glass balls around their nets to keep them afloat. And schoolchildren and office workers stained their fingers as they dipped their pens into the ubiquitous molded-glass inkwells that sat on every desk. While their original functions are obsolete, these evocative objects appeal to the creativity of collectors who see their many decorative possibilities.

nkwells

LEFT A tall blown-glass test tube has become an elegant vase that works as a perfect accessory to hold a bamboo stalk in a minimal interior.

RIGHT Blown-glass graduated beakers with finely etched numbers were part of a laboratory's basic equipment and were available in a wide range of sizes.

Blown-glass vacuum cups were widely used to treat various maladies until the 1950s, especially in Europe. A nice idea today is to use them as see-through bell jars for tiny collectibles such as pieces of coral, minerals, and shells.

LEFT These small blown-glass flasks were meant to test the quality of wine as it was maturing. The double-spouted beaker allowed for the decanting of liquids in the laboratory.

RIGHT A chunky blown-glass mortar and pestle, once an apothecary staple, can now crush spices in the kitchen.

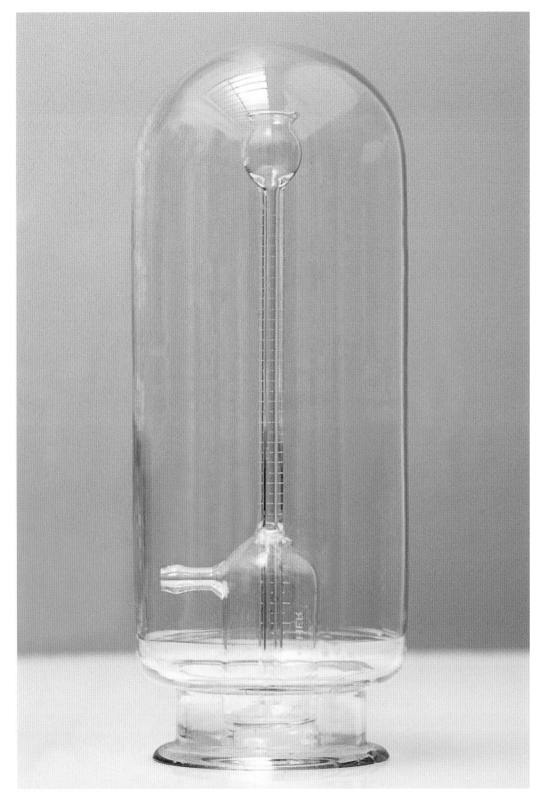

LEFT AND RIGHT New laboratory experiments at the end of the last century necessitated the creation of paraphernalia in extravagant shapes. Today, these blown-glass inventions are sought after and appreciated for their aesthetic qualities.

Colored and clear glass balls of
different shapes and sizes were
once attached to fishermen's
nets to help keep them afloat.
Now they catch rays of light
indoors, decoratively filling
rustic yet elegant wire baskets.

LEFT AND RIGHT Transformed into vases, perfectly spherical blown-glass balls that date from the second half of the eighteenth century were an aid to the crafts of lacemaking, watchmaking, and shoemaking in the era before electricity. At dusk, a lit candle was placed behind the sphere, which functioned as a magnifying glass and helped extend the craftsman's workday.

FAR LEFT Blue pressed-glass fire-extinguishing grenades are hard to find today, as they were meant to be destroyed. The shattered bottles released a gas that helped put out the fire.

LEFT A heavy pressed-glass insulator embossed Whitall Tatum Company No. 1 now functions as a paperweight.

BELOW FAR LEFT Patented in 1926 by the Master company of Litchfield, Illinois, this blow-molded glass bottle with its tin spout held a quart of gasoline.

BELOW LEFT The mold-blown ribbed bottle and inkwell are pieces of Sandwich Glass that date from about 1830.

RIGHT An amber-hued pressed-glass fire-extinguishing grenade has become a stylish vase.

FOLLOWING PAGES Molded-glass inkwells from the late nineteenth century, nostalgic today, came in a wide variety of shapes and sizes—not surprisingly, as everyone from schoolchildren to office workers needed them.

TO ENJOY

In any collector's search, there are certain glass objects that somehow present themselves as more singular, intimate, and personal. Taking pleasure in the surrounding world and being sensitive to the elements of light and water can enrich our daily lives. A beautiful, flower-filled glass bowl captures the light and transforms a corner of a room, while a summer house lit only by oil lamps and candlelit lanterns epitomizes romance. Both are the manifestation of a sense of well-being that has roots in the past. Made between 1840 and 1860, Sandwich Glass mold-blown cologne bottles—especially those in jewel-like colors that recalled the more sophisticated cut crystal versions from Bohemia—were popular and attested to a growing interest in pampering oneself. Today, some take pleasure not only in collecting but in using the fancy curvaceous bottles, while others prefer to adopt the simpler, cooler apothecary jars.

Vases
Apothecary Jars
Lanterns

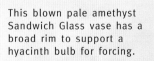

This blown pale amethyst Sandwich Glass vase has a broad rim to support a hyacinth bulb for forcing.

Luxuriant white hydrangeas are accommodated beautifully in a blow-molded goldfish bowl.

LEFT Cologne bottles that still retain their matching stoppers are much sought after by glass collectors. Pressed flint bottles in yellow, green, and cobalt blue, top row and bottom row, right, date from the mid-nineteenth century. Clear pressed-glass 1850s cologne bottles, bottom row, left, in the horn of plenty pattern, are marked H. E. Swan, a maker based in New Bedford, Massachusetts.

RIGHT Slender French opaline bottles catch the light in the vitrine of a New York bathroom

LEFT This huge pressed-glass bottle in the shape of a clock was designed to be a striking window display in an apothecary shop.

RIGHT Mid-nineteenth-century Sandwich Glass cologne bottles, like these examples in an amethyst hue, were blow-molded into graceful tapering shapes.

LEFT AND RIGHT Impressive three-piece flint-glass blow-molded show globes were made by companies such as the M'Kee Glass Company in Pittsburgh, Pennsylvania, in about 1860. Sometimes filled with colored liquids, they decorated the windows and shelves of apothecary shops.

ABOVE AND RIGHT In the past, pharmaceutical bottles and flasks held chemicals, acids, and herbal extracts in apothecary shops; today they are adapted to the modern bathroom.

Glass lanterns can provide a magical ambience. Examples include those used to celebrate France's Bastille Day on July 14, far left top and bottom, a pair of green blown lamps with handles from Provence, left bottom, and English Christmas lights, left top and right.

Cup-shaped glass votives in a rainbow of colors are hung on wire supports, one in the shape of a giant lyre, the other, a five-pointed star. Traditionally these illuminations were placed on the facades of French city halls in honor of Bastille Day.

ABOVE AND OPPOSITE Blown-glass oil lamps were made by the numerous glassblowers in the villages of Provence.

These colorless Sandwich Glass lamps, in which whale oil was burned, date from about 1830. Both have blown lead-glass bodies and pressed-glass bases. The lamp at left has a handle to allow it to be carried more easily from room to room.

These small, squat oil lamps,
typically used by shepherds in
southwestern France, have
molded-glass reservoirs,
cotton wicks, and wire harps
for carrying and hanging.

LEFT AND RIGHT These glass lanterns enhance an especially lovely setting, the rustic ambience of white-washed stone walls and weathered wood beams found in an old-fashioned Greek Islands house.

OPPOSITE The inhabitants of the French city of Lyons place these blown-glass processional lanterns outside their windows every year on December 8 to commemorate the end of a devastating plague.

ABOVE The pressed-glass cover of a Greek *kandilis*, or small church light, allows it to be used outdoors, even on windy days.

French blown or blow-molded glass fly-catchers were filled with sugary water and either placed on tables or hung outdoors in the trees. This old method of trapping pesky flies is still effective today.

AUSTRIA

Glass Museum (Lobmeyr)

1, Kärntner Strasse 26,
Vienna
Telephone: 43(1).512.05.08
The private glass museum of
Joseph Lobmeyer started in
1980. Includes Roman and
Venetian glass, as well as
examples from the Baroque,
Empire, and Biedermeier
periods.

BELGIUM

Musée Curtius
d' Archéologie et d'Art
décoratifs et Musée
du Verre

13 Quai de Maestricht
4000 Liège
Telephone: 32.4.221.94.04
One of the richest
collections in the world.
Includes Islamic and
Venetian glass, as well as
antique glass from the
Mediterranean region.

CZECHOSLOVAKIA

Czech Glass Museum - Glass
Works

Staromestské nám. 26
Prague 1
Telephone: 420.24.22.97.55

The museum exhibits a
history of glass production
in Bohemia.

Museum of Decorative Arts

17 Listopadu 2
11000 Prague 1
Telephone: 4.20(2).510.93111
The museum has a selection
of European and Czech crafts
of the sixteenth to the
nineteenth centuries,
including glassware,
ceramics, china, furniture,
metalwork, textiles, fashion
accessories, miniatures, and
book-related items.

ENGLAND

The British Museum

Great Russell Street
London WC1B3DG
Telephone: 44.207.323.8000
The museum includes
examples of domestic glass
from prehistory to the
twentieth century.

Broadfield House
Glass Museum

Barnett Lane
Kingswinford
West Midlands DY6 9NS
Telephone: 44.1384.812.745
www.dudley.gov.uk
The museum, with more than
12,000 pieces of British

glass from the seventeenth
century to the present day,
focuses on the achievements
of local Stourbridge
glassmakers.

Manchester City Art Gallery

Mosley Street
Manchester M60 2LA
Telephone: 44.161.234.1456
English and European glass
from the seventeenth to the
twentieth centuries.
Highlights include the
Tylecote collection of English
eighteenth-century drinking
glasses and nineteenth-
century Manchester pressed
glass.

Museum of London

150 London Wall
London ECZ 5HN
Telephone: 44.20.7600.3699
The museum exhibits glass
from domestic life in London
from Roman times onward,
including objects found in
archaeological excavations.

Sunderland Museum
and Art Gallery

Borough Road
Sunderland SR1 1PP
Telephone: 44.191.553.2323
The museum's collection
includes more than 1,000
pieces of Pyrex, as well as
American pressed glass and

examples made by three
local companies.

Victoria and Albert Museum

Cromwell Road
London SW7 2RL
Telephone: 44.20.7942.2000
A special gallery (no.131)
tells the story of glass from
ancient Egypt to the present
day.

Walker Art Gallery,
Craft and Design Dept.

William Brown Street
Liverpool L3 8EN
Telephone: 44.151.2070001
The Walker Art Gallery has a
large collection of
eighteenth-century drinking
glasses, as well as some
nineteenth-century and
twentieth-century pieces.
View by appointment.

FRANCE

Musée des Arts Décoratifs
Centre du Verre

Union Centrale des Arts
Décoratifs (UCAD)
107 rue de Rivoli
75001 Paris
Telephone: 33(1).44.55.58.53
The museum's glass
collection is displayed in the
glass department on the fifth
floor, which includes a

library and research facility dedicated to the study of French glass. The collection consists of many unique pieces as well as manufactured objects made for domestic use.

Musée des Arts Décoratifs
Hôtel de Lalande
39 rue Bouffard
33000 Bordeaux
Telephone: 33(5).56.00.72.51
www.mairie-bordeaux.fr
This varied collection of decorative arts from the Bordeaux region includes glass dating from the thirteenth to the nineteenth century.

Musée d'Unterlinden
1, rue Unterlinden
68 000 Colmar
Telephone: 33(3).89.20.15.50
www.museeunterlinden.com
The decorative arts collection highlights objects from rural and urban life of the Alsatian region, including glass dating from the Middle Ages to the Enlightenment.

Musée Adrien-Dubouche
8 bis, Place Winston Churchill
87000 Limoges
Telephone: 33(5).55.33.08.50
The museum has a

collection of more than 12,000 glass, porcelain, and faïence objects.

Musée des Beaux-Arts et de la Dentelle
12, rue du Capitaine Charles Aveline
6100 Alençon
Telephone: 33(2).33.32.40.07
www.ville-alencon.fr/vivre/musee.htm
The decorative arts collection was created from several prestigious private collections with objects dating from the seventeenth century to the beginning of the twentieth century.

Musée Centre des Arts
21, rue A.-Legros
76400 Fécamp
Telephone: 33(2).35.28.31.99
www.fecamp.com
The galleries on the first floor of the museum are dedicated to glass, porcelain, and faïence.

ITALY

The Museum of Glass
San Sebastiano
Piazza S. Sebastiano
17041 Altare
Telephone: 39.19.58.47.34
www1.elco.it/isvav

Altare has been a site of glassmaking since the thirteenth century. The museum's collection includes many important pieces, such as large hand-blown vases.

The Glass Museum
Palazzo Giustinian
Fondamenta Giustinian n. 8
Murano (Venice)
www.gomurano.com
Telephone: 39.41.739.586.
The only institution of its type in Italy, the Glass Museum now occupies Palazzo Giustinian, one of the largest palaces on the Lagoon. The "Museo Vetrario" is divided into three sections: archaeological glass, including Egyptian and Dalmatian examples; eighteenth- and nineteenth-century glass; and contemporary and industrial glass.

THE NETHERLANDS

Glass Museum
Lingedijk 28
4142 LD Leerdam
Telephone: 31.345.612714
www.royalleerdamcristal.nl
The museum displays famous Leerdam glass from the eighteenth century to the present.

SWITZERLAND

Musée Ariana – Musée Suisse de la céramique et du verre
10, Avenue de la Paix
12 02 Geneva
www.mah.ville-ge.ch
Telephone: 41.418.54.50
The Musée Ariana brings together several important Geneva-based collections and has become one of Europe's finest collections of Swiss-made glass.

UNITED STATES

The Bennington Museum
West Main Street
Bennington, Vermont 05201
Telephone: 802.447.1571
www.benningtonmuseum.com
The Bennington Museum's Pressed Glass Gallery includes hundreds of examples of early pressed glass, salt dishes, candlesticks, vases, and tableware, as well as a collection of 1,200 different patterns of goblets.

The Corning Museum of Glass
One Museum Way
Corning, New York 14830
Telephone: 877.SEE.CMOG or 607.974.8274
www.cmog.org

With more than 21,000 objects, the Corning Museum of Glass contains one of the most comprehensive collections of glass in the United States.

Frank J. Chiarenza Glass Museum
39 West Main Street
Meriden, Connecticut 06451
Telephone: 203.639.9778
The collection of more than 2,500 pieces of pressed and mold-blown glass includes many examples of milk glass.

Metropolitan Museum of Art
1000 Fifth Avenue
at 82nd Street
New York, New York 10028
General Information
Telephone: 212.535.7710
www.metmuseum.org
The Metropolitan Museum of Art's American collection has nearly 2,500 glass objects from the mid-eighteenth century through the early twentieth century. Strengths of the collection are many examples of pressed-pattern and blow-molded glass.

Museum of American Glass
1501 Glasstown Road
Millville, New Jersey 08332
Telephone: 609.825.6800
www.wheatonvillage.org

The Museum of American Glass includes more than 6,500 objects that are exhibited chronologically, beginning with a piece from the Wistarburgh Glass works, America's first successful glass factory.

Sandwich Historical Society and Glass Museum
129 Main Street
Town Hall Square
Route 130
Sandwich, Massachusetts 02563
Telephone: 508.888.0251
www.sandwichglassmuseum.org
In 1825, the Boston & Sandwich Glass Company built a glass factory in Sandwich, Cape Cod's oldest town. The museum displays 5,000 pieces of Sandwich glass.

RIGHT Pressed and blow-molded goblets and glasses are ready to be removed from the dishwasher.

OUR THANKS TO ALL THOSE WHO HAVE HELPED:
Gail Bardhan and Kristine Gable of the
Corning Museum of Glass, Lillian
Bassman, Jane Creech, Lester Dequaine
of the Dequaine Museum and Cultural
Center, Susan Friedman, Marike
Gauthier, Paul Himmel, Barbara
Hogenson, Brian Hynes, Maggie Katz,
Gregory Liakos of the Peabody Essex
Museums, Jean-Louis Menard, Paola
Navone, Nezka Pfeifer of the Sandwich
Glass Museum, Vincent Queau, Lazare
Rozenstroch, Matt Sarraf, Jonathan
Scott, Dan Shaw, Joan Vass, Carlese
Westock, and Egle Zygas of the
Metropolitan Museum of Art.

ALSO, AT HARRY N. ABRAMS, PUBLISHERS:
Paul Gottlieb, Mark Magowan,
Eric Himmel, Elisa Urbanelli, and
Michael Walsh.

Project Manager: Eric Himmel
Editor: Elisa Urbanelli
Designer: Stafford Cliff
Production artwork: Matt Sarraf

Library of Congress Cataloging-in-Publication Data
Slesin, Suzanne.
Everyday things : glass / Suzanne Slesin, Daniel Rozensztroch,
Stafford Cliff.
    p. cm.
  ISBN 0–8109–0620–1
1. Glassware–Catalogs. 2. Glass art–Catalogs. 3. Glass in interior
decoration–Catalogs. I. Rozensztroch, Daniel. II. Cliff, Stafford.
III. Title.   NK5104 .S56 2001
  748.2–dc21

                        2001003461

Printed and bound in Italy
10 9 8 7 6 5 4 3 2 1

Harry N. Abrams, Inc.
100 Fifth Avenue
New York, N.Y. 10011
www.abramsbooks.com

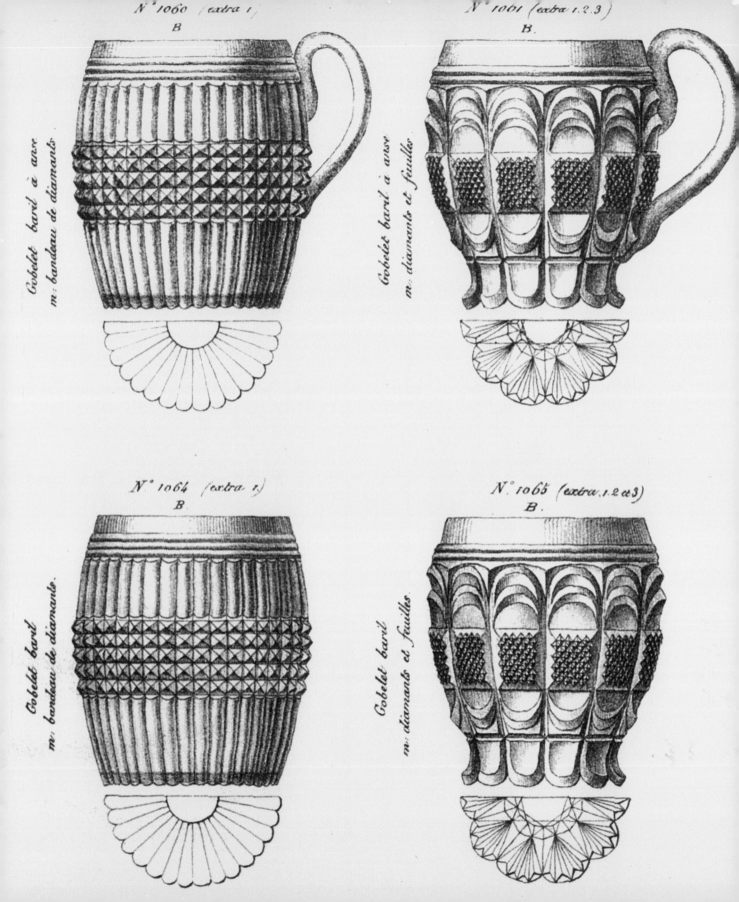

Nº 1060 (extra 1)
B

Gobelet baril à anse.
m: bandeau de diamants.

Nº 1061 (extra 1.2.3)
B.

Gobelet baril à anse.
m: diamants et feuilles.

Nº 1064 (extra 1)
B.

Gobelet baril.
m: bandeau de diamants.

Nº 1065 (extra 1.2 et 3)
B.

Gobelet baril.
m: diamants et feuilles.